PRESENTED TO

FROM

DATE

Inspiring Thoughts

Established 1912
100 Years of Excellence in Publishing
rajpal

₹ 150

ISBN : 9788170287490

INSPIRING THOUGHTS OF MAHATMA GANDHI

Compiled and edited by Meera Johri

Printed at Printed at Shiv Shakti Printers, Delhi

RAJPAL & SONS

1590, Madarsa Road, Kashmere Gate, Delhi-110006
Phone : 011-23869812, 23865483, 23867791
website : www.rajpalpublishing.com
e-mail : sales@rajpalpublishing.com
www.facebook.com/rajpalandsons

Inspiring Thoughts

MAHATMA GANDHI

Concept & Compilation by **Meera Johri**

rajpal

India is essentially *karmabhumi* (land of duty) in contradistinction to *bhogabhumi* (land of enjoyment)

The word Swaraj is a sacred word
a Vedic word
meaning self-rule and self-restraint
and not
freedom from all restraints
which 'independence' often means

For me
patriotism is the same as humanity
I am patriotic
because
I am human and humane
It is not exclusive

The highest form of freedom
carries with it
the greatest measure
of
discipline
and
humility

If the individual
ceases to count
what
is left of society

Not to have control over the senses
is like sailing in a
rudderless ship
bound to break to pieces
on coming in contact with
the very first rock

Realization of the goal
is
in exact proportion
to
that of the means
This is a proposition that admits
of
no exception

My Ahimsa would not tolerate
the idea of
giving a free meal to
a healthy person who
has not worked for it in
some honest way

Non-violence in its dynamic condition
means
conscious suffering
It does not mean
meek submission
to
thc will of
the evil doer
but it means
pitting of one's whole soul
against
the will of the tyrant

The kisan or the peasant
whether as a landless labourer
or
a labouring proprietor
comes first
He is the salt of the earth
which rightly belongs
or
should belong to him
not to the absentee landlord or
zamindar

Independence
must begin
at the bottom

Khadi to me
is the symbol of
unity of Indian humanity
of its
economic freedom
and
equality

Swadeshi is that spirit in us
which restricts us to the
use and service of
our immediate surroundings
to the
exclusion of
the more remote

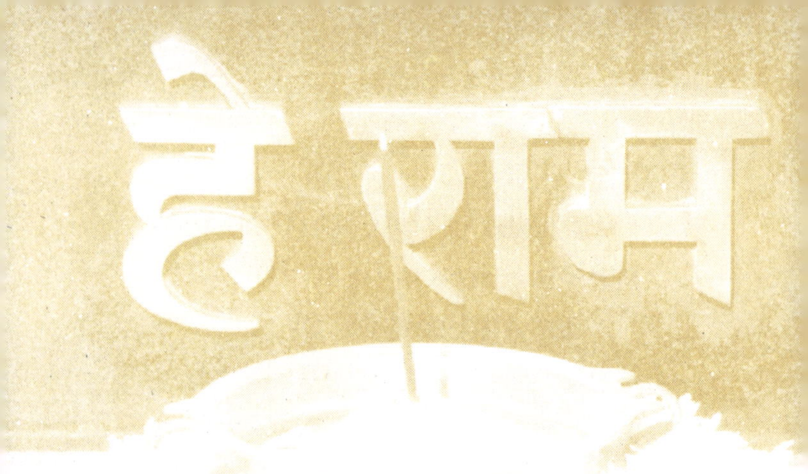

My patriotism is both
exclusive and inclusive
It is exclusive in the sense
that in all humility I confine
my attention to the land of my birth
But is inclusive in the sense
that my service is not
of a competitive or antognistic nature

Truth quenches untruth
love quenches anger
Self-suffering quenches violence
This eternal rule
is a rule not for saints only
but for all

Disease springs from a
wilful or ignorant
breach of the laws of nature
It follows therefore
that timely return to those laws
should mean restoration

Young men
claiming to be
the fathers of tomorrow
should be the salt of the nation
If
the salt loses its flavour
wherewith
shall it be salted

No culture can live
if it attempts
to be
exclusive

Our children must
from their infancy
be taught the dignity of labour

Literacy is not the end of education
nor even the beginning
It is only one of the means whereby
men and women can be educated
Literacy in itself
is
no education

Whenever you are
confronted with an opponent
conquer him
with love

One who has appreciated
the value of studies
is
a student
all his life

I am uncompromising in the matter
of women's rights
She should labour under no legal disability
not suffered by men
I should treat the
daughters and sons
on a footing of
pefect equality

The real property that a parent
can
transmit to all equally
is his or her character
and
educational facilities

A coward is
incapable of
exhibiting love
it is the perogative
of the brave

Culture of the mind
must be
subservient
to the heart

You can chain me
you can torture me
you can even destroy this body
but you will never
imprison my mind

Mass illiteracy is India's
sin and
shame
and
must be liquidated
The literacy campaign
must not
begin and end
with a knowledge of the alphabet
It must go hand in hand
with the spread
of useful knowledge

Untouchability
as it is practised in Hinduism today
is in my opinion
a sin against God and man
and is like a
poison slowly eating into the very
vitals of Hinduism
In my opinion
it has no sanction whatsoever
in the Hindu Shastras

Happiness is
when what you think
what you say
and
what you do
are in harmony

All religions proceed from
the same God
but all are imperfect
because they have come
down to us
through imperfect human
instrumentality

The bane of our life is our
exclusive provincialism
whereas
my province must be
co-extensive with the Indian boundary
so that ultimately it
extends to the
boundary of the earth
Else it perishes

In its inception
untouchability
was a rule of sanitation and
still is
in all parts of the world outside India
That is to say
an unclean person or thing is untouchable
but immediately
his or its
uncleanliness is shed
he or it is no longer untouchable

Religion is a personal matter
which should
have no place in politics

The newspaper press is a great power
but
just as an unchained torrent of water
submerges the whole countryside and
devastates crops
even so
an uncontrolled pen serves
but to destroy

It may be long before the
law of love
will be recognised in international affairs
The machineries of government
stand between
and hide the hearts
of one people
from
those of another

The remedy against cowardice
is not physical culture
but the braving of dangers

There will have to be rigid and iron discipline before we achieve anything great and enduring Discipline is learnt in the school of adversity

Those who claim
to lead the masses
must resolutely refuse
to be led by them

A leader is only first among equals

No school of thought can
claim a monopoly of right judgment
In a vast country like this
there must be room for
all schools of honest thought

I am convinced that the masses
do not want to fight
if
the leaders do not

If we do not account for
every single pie we receive
and do not make
judicious use of the funds
we shall deserve to be
blotted out of public life
Public money belongs to the
poor public of India

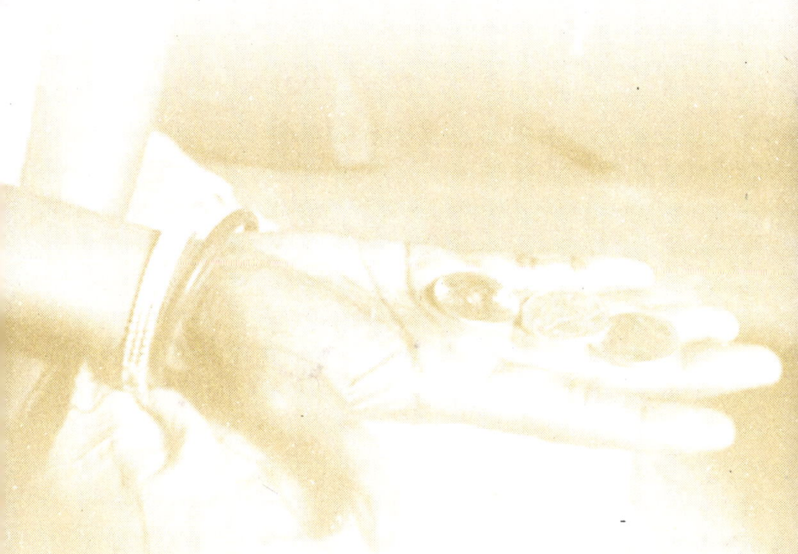

I have known the
serious consequences
overtaking
organizations that have counted
private character
as
a matter of no consequence

It would be a distinct gain
to
the national cause
if the leaders and workers
strictly
keep their hours

Action for one's own self binds
Action for the sake of others
delivers from bondage

What
is faith worth
if
it is not translated
into
action

Ahimsa is the highest ideal
It is meant for the brave
never for the cowardly

The greater the institution
the greater the chances of abuse
Democracy is a great institution
and therefore
liable to be greatly abused
The remedy is
not
avoidance of democracy
but
reduction of possibility of abuse
to a minimum

None low
none high
in the individual body
The head is not high
because it is the top of the body
nor are the soles of the feet low
because they touch the earth
Even as members of the
individual body are equal
so are the members of society
This is socialism

Every worthwhile accomplishment
big or little
has its stage of
drudgery and triumph
a beginning
a struggle
and
a victory

We should be ashamed of resting
or
having a square meal
so long as there is
one able-bodied
man or woman
without work or food

For the poor
the economic is the spiritual

Civilization
in the real sense of the term consists
not in the multiplication
but
in the deliberate and voluntary reduction
of wants
which promotes
real happiness and contentment
and
increases the capacity for service

True democracy cannot be
worked by
twenty men sitting at the centre
It has to be worked
from below
by
the people of every village

If everyone
whether rich or poor
has to take exercise
in some shape or form
why should it not
assume the form
of
productive bread labour?

The true source of rights is duty
If we all discharge our duties
rights will not be far to seek

Democracy is not a state in which
people act like sheep
Under democracy
individual liberty
of
opinion and action
is
jealously guarded

One man cannot do right
in one department of life
whilst
he is occupied in doing wrong
in any other department
Life is one indivisible whole

Economic equality is the master key
to
non-violent independence

There is more to life than
simply increasing
its speed

A born democrat
is
a born disciplinarian
Democracy comes naturally to him
who
is habituated normally
to
yield willing obedience
to all laws
human or divine

I do not draw any distinction
between
economics and ethics
Economics that hurt
the moral well-being
of an individual or a nation
are immoral
and
therefore sinful

Impure means result
in
an impure end

I look upon an increase in
the power of the State
with the greatest fear
Because although while
apparently doing good
by minimizing exploitation
it does the greatest harm to mankind
by destroying individuality
which lies at the root of all progress

Disobedience
to be civil
must be
sincere, respectful, restrained
never defiant
must be based upon
some well-understood principle
must not be capricious
and
above all
must have no ill-will or hatred behind it

We must identify ourselves
with the villagers
who toil under the hot sun
beating on their bent backs
and see
how we would like to
drink water from the pool
in which the villagers bathe
wash their clothes and pots
in which their cattle drink and roll
Then
and not till then
shall we truly represent the masses
and they will
as surely as I am writing this
respond to every call

I would say that if the village perishes
India will perish too
India will be no more India

There is a great deal of truth in
the saying that
man becomes what he eats
The grosser the food
the grosser the body

Even Swadeshi
like any other good thing
can be ridden to death
if it is made a fetish
That is a danger
that must be guarded against

An eye for an eye
makes the whole world
blind

When Panchayat Raj is established
public opinion will do
what violence
can never do

Khadi mentality means
decentralization of
the production and distribution
of
the necessaries of life

A man is
but the product of his thoughts
What he thinks
he
becomes

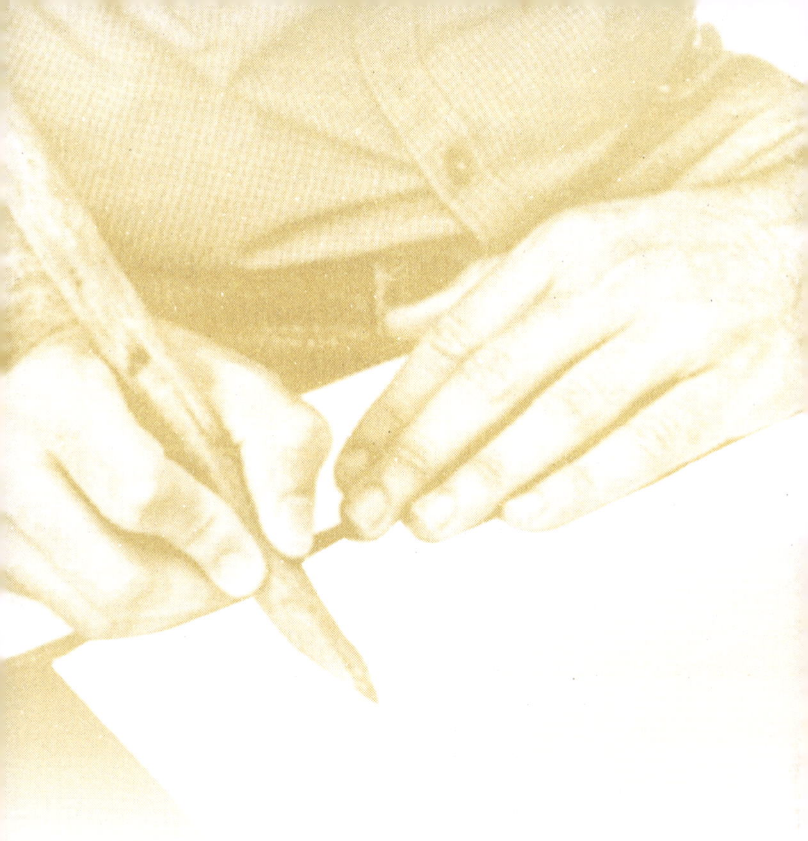

A man's real teacher is himself

Moral results can only be produced
by moral restraints
All other restraints
defeat the very purpose
for which they are intended

Why is there all this morbid
anxiety about female purity
Have women any say in the
matter of male purity
We hear nothing of women's
anxiety about men's chastity

The moment there is suspicion about
a person's motives
everything he does
becomes tainted

Hindus
if they want
unity among different races
must have the courage
to
trust the minorities

I…claim for the Charkha
the honour of being able
to solve the problem of
economic distress
in a most natural
simple, inexpensive and
business like manner

The only tyrant I accept in this world
is
the still voice within

Real education has to draw out the bes
from the boys and girls to be educated
This can never be done
by packing
ill-assorted and unwanted information
into the heads of the pupils
It becomes a dead weight
crushing all originality in them
and
turning them into mere automata

Free India will be no Hindu raj
It will be Indian raj based
not
on the majority of
any religious sect or community
but
on the representatives of the whole
people
without distinction of religion

The best way to find yourself
is to lose yourself
in the service of others

God
is
even though
the whole world
deny Him
Truth
stands
even if there be
no public support
It is self-sustained

We need a common language
not
in supersession of the vernaculars
but
in addition to them

The power of unarmed non-violence
is any day
far superior
to
that of
armed force

The strength to kill
is not essential to
self-defence
One ought to have the strength to die

As long as you derive
inner help
and
comfort
from anything
keep it

The weak can never forgive
Forgiveness
is the attribute of
the strong

Strength of numbers
is the delight of the timid
The valiant in spirit
glory in fighting alone

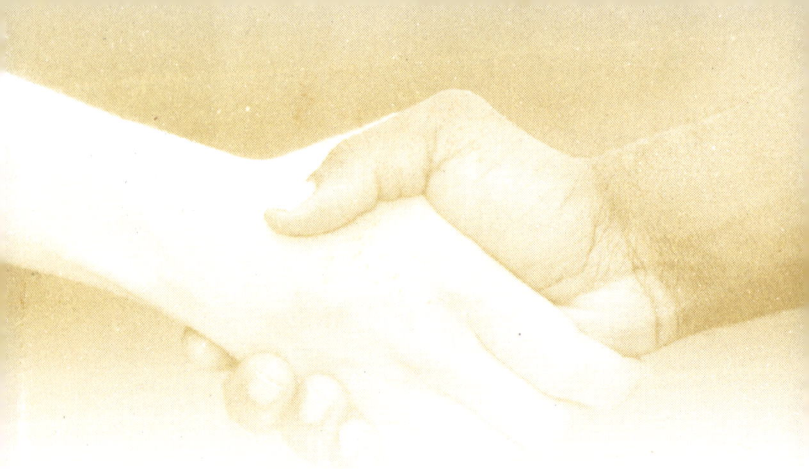

The sex education that I stand for
must have for its object
the conquest and sublimation of
the sex passion
Such education should
automatically
serve to bring home to children
the essential distinction between
man and brute

Satisfaction lies in the effort
not the attainment
Full effort
is
full victory

We must become the change we want to see

For me, the present is merged
in eternity
I may not sacrifice
the latter for the present

Anger
and
intolerance
are the twin enemies of
correct understanding

Strength
does not come
from
physical capacity
It comes
from
an indomitable will

A 'No'
uttered from the deepest conviction
is better than
a 'Yes'
merely uttered to please
or worse
to avoid trouble

A religion that takes no account
of practical affairs
and
does not help to solve them
is
no religion

As human beings
our greatness lies not so much
in being able to remake the world
as in being able to
remake ourselves